Pro Femina

a poem by

Carolyn Kizer

With a note by the author

BkMk Press
University of Missouri–Kansas City

The author wishes to acknowledge the editors of *Encounter, The Carleton Miscellany, Antæus,* and *The Yale Review,* where parts of *Pro Femina* first appeared.

Cover art from *Wallpaper* by Charles Dana Gibson (1902)
Book design by Roxanne Witt

The Roy Fox Memorial Chapbook Series is in memory of Roy Fox, a founder of BkMk Press.

BkMk Press
University of Missouri-Kansas City
5100 Rockhill Road
Kansas City, Missouri 64110
(816) 235-2558
bkmk@umkc.edu

Library of Congress Cataloging-in-Publication Data

Kizer, Carolyn.
    Pro femina / by Carolyn Kizer.
      p. cm. – (Roy Fox memorial chapbook series ; #4)
    ISBN 1-886157-30-8
    1.   Women—Poetry. I. Title. II. Series.

PS3521.I9 P76 1999
811'.54—dc21
                                   99-055557

1   2   3   4   5   6   7   8   9   10

Printed by Walsworth, Marceline, MO.

Contents

Author's Note — v

One — 7

Two — 9

Three — 11

Four : Fanny — 14

Five : The Erotic Philosophers — 18

Author's Note

I wrote the first three sections of *Pro Femina* in a state of high excitement after reading the English translation of *The Second Sex* in 1953. Mlle. de Beauvoir elucidated and confirmed so many thoughts I had had about women's condition. It is one of the great moments in life when you realize that you are not alone, and that your feelings are not unique, but shared by another. One usually impercipient critic—and a woman at that!—said that I covered my pain with bluster, which infuriated me because I had been so happy writing *Pro Femina*. But many things have changed for the better in the last thirty-five years, including criticism of and by women.

Another characteristic response at the time was in the group of writers—all men except for me—who met irregularly at my house to discuss our work. They saw nothing of value in *Pro Femina*, nothing at all; and I was quite discouraged until Rolfe Humphries and Robert Fitzgerald came to town and praised the work. Bless their ghosts! "From Pro Femina" was published in *Encounter* (in its pre-C.I.A.-sponsored days, I hasten to add) and after being rejected by most of the leading American literary magazines of the day, in *The Carleton Miscellany,* edited by my friend Reed Whittemore, in 1954. Mail poured in from women, mostly young women. A number of them questioned the lines, ". . . and the luck of our husbands and lovers, who keep free women." I developed quite a little lecture on irony and paradox in response to these puzzled girls!

I was also frequently asked why I had called the work "From Pro Femina." I had a feeling that I wasn't through with the subject, and so it turned out. Twenty years later I wrote "Fanny," published in *Antæus* (I'm getting respectable!) and in my book *YIN* (1984). It's the story of a woman of fiery intelligence and baulked creativity, who devoted crucial years of her life to caring for that near-genius and near-invalid, Robert Louis Stevenson, keeping him alive, as she said, for eight more years. After he died she blossomed forth as a writer. It was her book, *Our Samoan Adventure*, which prompted me to write "Fanny," and from which I borrowed shamelessly and copiously. Fanny Stevenson, in my mind, stood for generations of women who selflessly served men—fathers, sons and lovers—until their loss enabled these women to blossom as artists themselves. Before their liberation, their willing servitude, they found other ways of expressing themselves. In Fanny's case it was the outdoors in Samoa, digging in the earth, planting. (For some time the poem was called "Planting.") In my book *Mermaids in the Basement: Poems for Women* (1984), I incorporated "Fanny" into *Pro Femina*.

I spent the year 1997-1998 writing "The Erotic Philosophers" about the attitudes of St. Augustine and Kierkegaard towards women. I concentrated wholly on this long poem, writing nothing else during those long months of composition and revision. This poem, too, had a rocky beginning with editors, rejected by *The Paris Review* and *Poetry*, whose editor said he wasn't sure it was a poem. Then it was promptly accepted by *The Yale Review* after I'd had another crisis of confidence. It was picked out by Robert Bly and David Lehman for *The Best American Poetry 1999*. In the commentary for that volume I ended by saying, " I think of adding this poem as the end piece to perhaps my best-known work, *Pro Femina*, and finishing it once and for all. Although its ending seems a bit pallid and submissive for an old ironclad feminist like me." And so it has come to pass. I really think it's completed, but a new century is in the offing, and who knows? . . .

Carolyn Kizer

One

From Sappho to myself, consider the fate of women.
How unwomanly to discuss it! Like a noose or an albatross
   necktie
The clinical sobriquet hangs us: cod-piece coveters.
Never mind these epithets; I myself have collected some honeys.
Juvenal set us apart in denouncing our vices
Which had grown, in part, from having been set apart:
Women abused their spouses, cuckolded them, even plotted
To poison them. Sensing, behind the violence of his manner—
"Think I'm crazy or drunk?"—his emotional stake in us,
As we forgive Strindberg and Nietzsche, we forgive all those
Who cannot forget us. We *are* hyenas. Yes, we admit it.

While men have politely debated free will, we have howled for it,
Howl still, pacing the centuries, tragedy heroines.
Some who sat quietly in the corner with their embroidery
Were Defarges, stabbing the wool with the names of their ancient
Oppressors, who ruled by the divine right of the male—
I'm impatient of interruptions! I'm aware there were millions
Of mutes for every Saint Joan or sainted Jane Austen,
Who, vague-eyed and acquiescent, worshiped God as a man.
I'm not concerned with those cabbageheads, not truly feminine
But neutered by labor. I mean real women, like *you* and like *me*.

Freed in fact, not in custom, lifted from furrow and scullery,
Not obliged, now, to be the pot for the annual chicken,
Have we begun to arrive in time? With our well-known
Respect for life because it hurts so much to come out with it;
Disdainful of "sovereignty," "national honor" and other
    abstractions;
We can say, like the ancient Chinese to successive waves
    of invaders,
"Relax, and let us absorb you. You can learn temperance
In a more temperate climate." Give us just a few decades
Of grace, to encourage the fine art of acquiescence
And we might save the race. Meanwhile, observe our
    creative chaos,
Flux, efflorescence—whatever you care to call it!

Two

I take as my theme "The Independent Woman,"
Independent but maimed: observe the exigent neckties
Choking violet writers; the sad slacks of stipple-faced matrons;
Indigo intellectuals, crop-haired and callous-toed,
Cute spectacles, chewed cuticles, aced out by full-time beauties
In the race for a male. Retreating to drabness, bad manners
And sleeping with manuscripts. Forgive our transgressions
Of old gallantries as we hitch in chairs, light our own cigarettes,
Not expecting your care, having forfeited it by trying to get even.

But we need dependency, cosseting and well-treatment.
So do men sometimes. Why don't they admit it?
We will be cows for a while, because babies howl for us,
Be kittens or bitches, who want to eat grass now and then
For the sake of our health. But the role of pastoral heroine
Is not permanent, Jack. We want to get back to the meeting.
Knitting booties and brows, tartars or termagants, ancient
Fertility symbols, chained to our cycle, released
Only in part by devices of hygiene and personal daintiness,

Strapped into our girdles, held down, yet uplifted by man's
Ingenious constructions, holding coiffures in a breeze,
Hobbled and swathed in whimsey, tripping on feminine
Shoes with fool heels, losing our lipsticks, you, me,
In ephemeral stockings, clutching our handbags and packages.
Our masks, always in peril of smearing or cracking,
In need of continuous check in the mirror or silverware,
Keep us in thrall to ourselves, concerned with our surfaces.
Look at man's uniform drabness, his impersonal envelope!
Over chicken wrists or meek shoulders, a formal, hard-fibered
    assurance.
The drape of the male is designed to achieve self-forgetfulness.

So, Sister, forget yourself a few times and see where it gets you:
Up the creek, alone with your talent, sans everything else.
You can wait for the menopause, and catch up on your reading.
So primp, preen, prink, pluck and prize your flesh,
All posturings! All ravishment! All sensibility!
Meanwhile, have you used your mind today?
What pomegranate raised you from the dead,
Springing, full-grown, from your own head, Athena?

Three

I will speak about women of letters, for I'm in the racket.
Our biggest successes to date? Old maids to a woman.
And our saddest conspicuous failures? The married spinsters
On loan to the husbands they treated like surrogate fathers.
Think of that crew of self-pitiers, not-very-distant,
Who carried the torch for themselves and got first-degree burns.
Or the sad sonneteers, toast-and-teasdales we loved at thirteen;
Middle-aged virgins seducing the puerile anthologists
Through lust-of-the-mind; barbiturate-drenched Camilles
With continuous periods, murmuring softly on sofas
When poetry wasn't a craft but a sickly effluvium,
The air thick with incense, musk, and emotional blackmail.

I suppose they reacted from an earlier womanly modesty
When too many girls were scabs to their stricken sisterhood,
Impugning our sex to stay in good with the men,
Commencing their insecure bluster. How they must have
    swaggered
When women themselves endorsed their own inferiority!
Vestals, vassals and vessels, rolled into several,
They took notes in rolling syllabics, in careful journals,
Aiming to please a posterity that despises them.
But we'll always have traitors who swear that a woman surrenders

Her Supreme Function, by equating Art with aggression
And failure with Femininity. Still, it's just as unfair
To equate Art with Femininity, like a prettily-packaged
    commodity
When we are the custodians of the world's best-kept secret:
Merely the private lives of one-half of humanity.

But even with masculine dominance, we mares and mistresses
Produced some sleek saboteuses, making their cracks
Which the porridge-brained males of the day were too thick to
    perceive,
Mistaking young hornets for perfectly harmless bumblebees.
Being thought innocuous rouses some women to frenzy;
They try to be ugly by aping the ways of the men
And succeed. Swearing, sucking cigars and scorching
    the bedspread,
Slopping straight shots, eyes blotted, vanity-blown
In the expectation of glory: *she writes like a man!*
This drives other women mad in a mist of chiffon.
(One poetess draped her gauze over red flannels, a practical
    feminist.)

But we're emerging from all that, more or less,
Except for some lady-like laggards and Quarterly priestesses
Who flog men for fun, and kick women to maim competition
Now, if we struggle abnormally, we may almost seem normal;
If we submerge our self-pity in disciplined industry;
If we stand up and be hated, and swear not to sleep with editors;

If we regard ourselves formally, respecting our true limitations
Without making an unseemly show of trying to unfreeze our
   assets;
Keeping our heads and our pride while remaining unmarried;
And if wedded, kill guilt in its tracks when we stack up the dishes
And defect to the typewriter. And if mothers, believe in the luck
   of our children,
Whom we forbid to devour us, whom we shall not devour,
And the luck of our husbands and lovers, who keep free women.

Four : Fanny

At Samoa, hardly unpacked, I commenced planting,
When I'd opened the chicken crates, built the Cochins a coop.
The Reverend Mr. Claxton called, found me covered with mud,
My clothes torn, my hair in a wad, my bare feet bleeding.
I had started the buffalo grass in the new-made clearing.
The next day the priest paid a visit. Civil but restless,
I was dying to plant the alfalfa seed—gave him a packet.

That evening I paced up and down, dropping melon seeds,
Tomatoes and bush lima beans here and there
Where I thought they would grow. We were short of food now,
So I cooked up a mess of fat little parrots, disturbed
At the way they suggested cages and swings and stands . . .
An excellent meal. I have been told the dodo survived here,
And yearn for a pet on a string. And I built the pig-house.

I had brought sweet coconut seed from Savage Island.
I planted kidney potatoes in small earthen hills.
Sowed seeds of eggplant in numerous boxes of soil,
Tomato and artichoke too; half-a-dozen fine pineapple
Sent over by Mr. Carruthers, the island solicitor.
As fast as we eat them, we plant the tops.
The kitchen a shack near the house. I made bread in the rain.

October, 1890. I have been here nearly a month;
Put in corn, peas, onions, radishes, lettuce. Lima beans
Are already coming up. The ripening cantaloupe were stolen.
Carruthers gave me mint root and grenadilla
Like a bouquet; he delivered a load of trees,
Two mangoes among them. I set them out in a heavy rain,
Then rounded off the afternoon sowing Indian corn.

Louis has called me a peasant. How I brooded!
Confided it to you, diary, then crossed it out.
Peasant because I delve in the earth, the earth I own.
Confiding my seed and root—I too a creator?
My heart melts over a bed of young peas. A blossom
On the rose tree is like a poem by my son.
My hurt healed by its cause, I go on planting.

No one else works much. The natives take it easy;
The colonials keep their shops, and a shortage of customers.
The mail comes four times a month, and the gossip all day.
The bars are crowded with amateur politicians,
Office-seekers I named the earwig consul and king:
Big talkers, with small-time conspirators drinking them in.
Mr. Carruthers and I picked a site for the kitchen garden.

I was planting a new lot of corn and pumpkin
When a young chief arrived, laden with pineapple plants.
I set them out as I talked to him on the way home.
Rats and a wild hen ate the corn. Lettuce got too much sun.

So I dug a new patch up the road; in the fragrant evening
I confided to Louis, a puff of the sweetest scent
Blows back as I cast away a handful of so-called weeds!

It still hurts, his remark that I have the soul of a peasant.
My vanity, like a newly-felled tree, lies prone and bleeding.
I clear the weeds near the house for planting maize.
Sweet corn and peas are showing. I send for more seeds.
I clean out the potatoes, which had rotted in their hills.
Of course, RLS is not idle; he is writing *A Footnote to History:*
How the great powers combine to carve up these islands.

I discovered the ylang-ylang tree: a base for perfume,
Though it suggested to me the odor of boots.
Another tree is scented like pepper and spice,
And one terrible tree, I am forced to say,
Smells like ordure . . . It nearly made me ill.
Breadfruit is plentiful. I found a banana grove,
Began clearing it instantly, and worked till I was dizzy.

The garden looks like a graveyard: beds shaped like tombs.
I plant cabbage which I loathe, so the British won't tease me
For not growing it. But behold! In the hedge
Among citron and lime, many lemon trees, in full bearing.
Still, I will fall to brooding before the mirror,
Though Louis says he finds the peasant class "interesting."
He is forty today. I am ten years his senior.

On the cleared land, the green mummy-apple,
Male and female, is springing up everywhere.
I discover wild ginger, turmeric, something like sugar.
Roots of orange, breadfruit and mango, seeds of cacao
Came with a shipment from Sydney; also eleven
Young navel orange trees. The strawberry plants are rotten.
I am given a handul of bees. I plant more pineapple.

All fall I am cursed with asthma, rheumatics, a painful ear.
Christmas. A hurricane. And the New Year begins.
Louis describes it divinely to Henry James.
Mr. Carruthers' gift pineapple starts to fruit.
I set out one precious rhubarb plant, pause to gloat
At the ripe tomatoes, the flourishing long-podded beans.
But the neighbors' horses break in and trample the corn.

Sometimes, when planting, a strange subterranean rumble
—Volcanic?—vexes the earth beneath this peasant haunch.
I rise up from my furrow, knuckle smooth my brow
As I sniff the air, suddenly chemical, a sulphurous fume.
Louis insisted on going to Sydney, fell ill again.
His mother comes back with him, finds me on my knees.
The old lady's heart leaps! Alas, I am planting, not praying.

We both rise at five-thirty, after dreaming of weeds.
Louis describes to me endless vivid deeps:
Dreams of nettle-stings, stabs from the citron's thorns,
The ants' fiery bites, the resistance of mud and slime,

The evasions of wormy roots, the dead weight of heat
In the sudden puffs of air . . . Louis writes till nine,
Then if he's well enough, he helps with the weeding.

He writes Colvin, keeper of prints at the British Museum,
"I know pleasure still . . . with a thousand faces,
None perfect, a thousand tongues, all broken,
A thousand hands, all with scratching nails . . ."
"High among joys, I place this delight of weeding,
Out here alone by the garrulous water, under the silence
Of the high wind, broken by sounds of birds."

The shock of bird-calls, laughing and whistling!
They mimic his name till it seems, he says,
"The birds re-live the business of my day."
But the rain continues to fall on birds and weeds.
The new servants fooled around with the ice machine
As the house leaked and listed. Mildew spread its failure.
Mrs. S. gave me some nuts, and went back to Australia.

Green peppers, eggplant, tomatoes are flourishing,
Asparagus also. The celery does to season soup.
Avocados grow at a rate that is almost frightening.
Coconuts too. I read about Stanley and Livingstone.
I cured my five ulcers with calomel, wished I could tell
Stanley the remedy. Instead, I made perfume.
The servants feared devils, so I planted the orange grove alone.

For two months I misplaced this diary . . .
War is in the air, talk of killing all whites.
I bought coffee trees, rose trees and Indian beans,
Then went to Fiji to rest, and to get more seeds
From a former Kew gardener. An Indian in a shop
Told me how to raise Persian melon and cauliflower
And a radish that turns into a turnip when it grows up.

I came home to a burgeoning world: cacao, custard squash.
The new house was finished, and painted peacock blue.
The jealous old cat bit off the new cat's toes.
My mother-in-law returned with her Bible and lady's maid;
My daughter, her family, and my son Lloyd came too.
The relatives had a terrible row. Mrs. S. refused
To pray with the servants. I throw up my hands!

My diary entries grow farther and farther apart.
I wrote life was a strain. Later, someone crossed it out.
In pain again, from an aneurysm inside my head . . .
I planted more and more cacao, and a form of cherry tree,
Tobacco and rubber, taught how by Mr. Sketchley.
I planted more cacao through an epidemic of 'flu.
Three hundred seeds in baskets broke through the ground.

I get almost no time to write. I have been planting . . .
Four kinds of cabbage are doing very well.
Mr. Haggard, the land commissioner, come to dine,

Points out a weed which makes excellent eating
Cooked like asparagus. I shall try it very soon.
Now, when the Reverend Mr. Claxton comes to call,
I refuse to see him. I am tired of the Claxtons.

The political situation grows grim. I rage at Louis
Who toasts, "Her Blessed Majesty the Queen," then aggressively
Throbbing, turns to my American son
To say he may drink to the President *afterwards*
If he likes. I am writing this down
Hoping Louis will see it later, and be ashamed
Of his childishness and bad taste. (This will be erased.)

Because war is near, the Germans stop growing cacao.
Captain Hufnagel offers me all the seeds I can use.
So now we are blazing with cacao fever,
The whole family infected. Six hundred plants set out!
The verandah tracked with mud, and the cacao litter.
Mrs. S. upset by the mess. Twelve hundred cacaos planted.
Joe, my son-in-law, planted his thousandth tree today.

The tree onions make large bulbs but don't want to seed.
Most vigorous: sunflower, watermelon—weeds!
The jelly from berries out of the bush is delicious;
Lovely perfume from massoi, citron, vanilla and gum.
The peanuts are weeded while Joe plays on his flute.
I plant cabbage by moonlight, set out more cacao.
The heart of a death's-head moth beats a tattoo in my hand.

Planted coffee all day, and breadfruit, five beauties . . .
Planted coffee the better part of the day, eight plants.
In the nursery, three times that many. Planted coffee . . .
Painted the storm shutters. Planted coffee all morning.
I found a heap of old bones in a bush near the sty;
Two heads and a body: a warrior died with his prize.
Louis gave the bones a funeral and a burial.

A series of hurricanes: Louis writes to *The Times*
Of "the foul colonial politics." I send to New York for seeds:
Southern Cross cabbage, eggplant, sweet potato
And two thousand custard apples. Louis' own seed,
David Balfour, is growing. I wrote nothing
From June till the end of this year; too busy planting.
The Samoan princes are getting nearer to war.

It pains me to write this: my son-in-law has gone native
In a spectacular way. Belle is divorcing him.
Austin, my grandson, is in school in Monterey.
I have not, I believe, mentioned Mrs. Stevenson recently.
She has gone back to Scotland. The first breadfruit bore.
Belle and I go on sketching expeditions
To the hostile Samoan camps, stop in town for ginger beer.

Mr. Haggard begged us to stay in town
Because he bitterly wanted women to protect.
I suggested to him that I and my daughter
Could hide under his table and hand him cartridges

At the window, to complete the romantic effect.
It is clear that Mr. Haggard is Ryder's brother!
He said, "You'd sell your life for a bunch of banana trees."

I've given permission to most of the "boys"
To go to the races. Lloyd has put up the lawn tennis things.
Mr. Gurr, the neighbor, rushes in to say war has begun.
We all race to the mission. Eleven heads have been taken.
Later: Mr. Dine's cousin received a head smeared with black
(The custom is to return them to the bereaved).
He washed it off and discovered it was his brother.

He sat there, holding his brother's head in his hands,
Kissing it, bathing it with his tears. A scandal arose
Because the heads of three girls have been taken as well
(unheard of before in Samoa), returned wrapped in silk
    to their kin.
At Malie, the warriors danced a head-hunter's pantomime;
The men who had taken heads carried great lumps of raw pork
Between their teeth, cut in the semblance of heads.

I stopped writing this. Too hysterical with migraine.
Also, people find where I hide it, and strike things out.
Our favorite chief is exiled for life. The war winds down.
Louis works on his masterpiece, *The Weir of Hermiston.*
Well. I've kept him alive for eight more years,

While his dear friends would have condemned him to fog
    and rain
So they might enjoy his glorious talk in London,

Though it be the end of him. Fine friends! Except for James.
Later: At six, Louis helped with the mayonnaise,
When he put both hands to his head, said, "Oh, what a pain!
Do I look strange?" I said no, not wanting to frighten him.
He was never conscious again. In two hours he died.
Tonight, the chiefs with their axes are digging a path
To the top of the mountain. They will dig his grave.

I will leave here as soon as I can, and never return,
Except to be buried beside him. I will live like a gipsy
In my wild, ragged clothes, until I am old, old.
I will have pretty gardens wherever I am,
But never breadfruit, custard apples, grenadilla, cacao,
Pineapple, ylang-ylang, citron, mango, cacao,
Never again succumb to the fever of planting.

Five : The Erotic Philosophers

It's a spring morning; sun pours in the window
As I sit here drinking coffee, reading Augustine.
And finding him, as always, newly minted
From when I first encountered him in school.
Today I'm overcome with astonishment
At the way we girls denied all that was mean
In those revered philosophers we studied;
Who found us loathsome, loathsomely seductive;
Irrelevant at best to noble discourse
Among the sex, the only sex that counted.
Wounded, we pretended not to mind it
And wore tight sweaters to tease our shy professor.

We sat in autumn sunshine "as the clouds arose
From slimy desires of the flesh, and from
Youth's seething spring." Thank you, Augustine.
Attempting to seem blasé, our cheeks on fire
It didn't occur to us to rush from the room
Instead, we brushed aside "the briars of unclean desire"
And struggled on through mires of misogyny
Till we arrived at Kierkegaard, and began to see

That though Saint A. and Søren had much in common
Including fear and trembling before women.
The Saint scared himself, while Søren was scared of *us*.
Had we, poor girls, been flattered by their thralldom?

Yes, it was always us, the rejected feminine
From whom temptation came. It was our flesh
With its deadly sweetness that led them on.
Yet how could we not treasure Augustine,
"Stuck fast in the birdlime of pleasure"?
That roomful of adolescent poets manqué
Assuaged, bemused by music, let the meaning go.
Swept by those psalmic cadences, we were seduced!
Some of us tried for awhile to be well-trained souls
And pious seekers, enmeshed in the Saint's dialectic:
Responsible for our actions, yet utterly helpless.
A sensible girl would have barked like a dog before God.

We students, children still, were shocked to learn
The children these men desired were younger than we!
Augustine fancied a girl about eleven,
The same age as Adeodatus, Augustine's son.
Søren, like Poe, eyed his girl before she was sixteen,
To impose his will on a malleable child, when
She was not equipped to withstand or understand him.
Ah, the Pygmalion instinct! Mold the clay!

Create the compliant doll that can only obey,
Expecting to be abandoned, minute by minute.
It was then I abandoned philosophy,
A minor loss, although I majored in it.

But we were a group of sunny innocents.
I don't believe we knew what evil meant.
Now I live with a well-trained soul who deals with evil
Including error, material or spiritual,
Easily, like changing a lock on the kitchen door.
He prays at set times and in chosen places
(at meals, in church), while I
Pray without thinking how or when to pray,
In a low mumble, several times a day,
Like running a continuous low fever;
The sexual impulse for the most part being over.
Believing I believe. Not banking on it ever.

It's afternoon. I sit here drinking kir
And reading Kierkegaard: "All sin begins with fear."
(True. We lie first from terror of our parents.)
In, I believe, an oblique crack at Augustine,
Søren said by denying the erotic
It was brought to the attention of the world.
The rainbow curtain rises on the sensual:
Christians must admit it before they can deny it.

He reflected on his father's fierce repression
Of the sexual, which had bent him out of shape;
Yet he had to pay obeisance to that power:
He chose his father when he broke with Regina.

Søren said by denying the erotic
It is brought to the attention of the world.
You must admit it before you can deny it.
So much for "Repetition"—another theory
Which some assume evolved from his belief
He could replay his courtship of Regina
With a happy ending. Meanwhile she'd wait for him,
Eternally faithful, eternally seventeen.
Instead, within two years, the bitch got married.
In truth, he couldn't wait till he got rid of her,
To create from recollection, not from living;
To use the material, not the material girl.

I sip my kir, thinking of *Either/Or*,
Especially *Either*, starring poor Elvira.
He must have seen *Giovanni* a score of times,
And Søren knew the score.
He took Regina to the opera only once,
And as soon as Mozart's overture was over,
Kierkegaard stood up and said, "Now we are leaving.
You have heard the best: the expectation of pleasure."

In his interminable aria on the subject
SK insisted the performance *was* the play.
Was the overture then the foreplay? Poor Regina
Should have known she'd be left waiting in the lurch.

Though he chose a disguise in which to rhapsodize
It was his voice too: Elvira's beauty
Would perish soon; the deflowered quickly fade:
A night-blooming cereus after Juan's one-night stand.
Søren, eyes clouded by romantic mist,
Portrayed Elvira always sweet sixteen.
SK's interpretation seems naive.
He didn't realize that innocent sopranos
Who are ready to sing Elvira, don't exist.
His diva may have had it off with Leporello
Just before curtain time, believing it freed her voice
(so backstage legend has it), and weakened his.

I saw La Stupenda sing Elvira once.
Her cloak was larger than an army tent.
Would Giovanni be engulfed when she inhaled?
Would the boards shiver when she stamped her foot?
Her voice of course was great. Innocent it was not.
Søren, long since, would have fallen in a faint.
When he, or his doppelgänger, wrote
That best-seller, *The Diary of a Seducer,*
He showed how little he knew of true Don Juans:
Those turgid letters, machinations and excursions,
Those tedious conversations with dull aunts,
Those convoluted efforts to get the girl!

Think of the worldly European readers
Who took Søren seriously, did not see
His was the cynicism of the timid virgin.
Once in my youth I knew a real Don Juan
Or he knew me. He didn't need to try,
The characteristic of a true seducer.

He seems vulnerable, shy; he hardly speaks.
Somehow you know he will never speak of you.
You trust him—and you thrust yourself at him.
He responds with an almost absent-minded grace.
Even before the consummation he's looking past you
For the next bright yearning pretty face.

Relieved at last of anxieties and tensions
When your terrible efforts to capture him are over,
You overflow with happy/unhappy languor.
But SK's alter ego believes the truly terrible
Is for you to be consoled by the love of another.
We women, deserted to a woman, have a duty
Rapidly to lose our looks, decline and die,
Our only chance of achieving romantic beauty.
So Augustine was sure, when Monica, his mother,
Made him put aside his nameless concubine
She'd get her to a nunnery, and pine.
He chose his mother when he broke with his beloved.

In Søren's long replay of his wrecked romance,
"Guilty/Not Guilty," he says he must tear himself away
From earthly love, and suffer to love God.
Augustine thought better; love, human therefore flawed,
Is the way to the love of God. To deny this truth
Is to be "left outside, breathing into the dust,
Filling the eyes with earth," We women,
Outside, breathing dust, are still the Other.
The evening sun goes down; time to fix dinner.
"You women have no major philosophers." We know.
But we remain philosophic, and say with the Saint,
"Let me enter my chamber and sing my songs of love."

About the Author

Carolyn Kizer was born in Spokane in 1925, educated at Sarah Lawrence College (B.A.) and Columbia University (Chinese Cultural Fellow). She spent a year in China, and twenty years later, a year in Pakistan. With Richard Hugo she founded the quarterly *Poetry Northwest*, which she edited until going as first Director of Literature for the National Endowment for the Arts, from 1965 until 1970, when she resigned after the Chairman of the N.E.A., Roger Stevens, was fired by President Nixon. She then went to the University of North Carolina, where she reorganized the poetry program. She resigned to marry the architect and city planner, John M. Woodbridge, F.A.I.A., and lived in Washington, D.C., until 1977, when she and her husband removed to Berkeley, California. She has taught at many universities, including Columbia, Princeton and Stanford. Her book of poems, *YIN*, won the Pulitzer Prize in 1985. She has received other honors and awards from the National Academy, the Poetry Society of America and the Theodore Roethke Foundation. She was made a Chancellor of the Academy of American Poets in 1995 but resigned four years later because of the Chancellors' neglect of ethnic and geographic diversity—a situation since greatly improved. She has published seven books of poetry, two books of criticism and a book of translations. She edited *The Essential John Clare* and *100 Great Poems by Women*. Her most recent book is *Harping On: Poems 1985-1995*. She has three children by her first husband, three stepchildren and five grandchildren. She and her husband live in Sonoma, California, and spend part of each year in Paris.